Notes
To My
Daughters

Rene Salzman

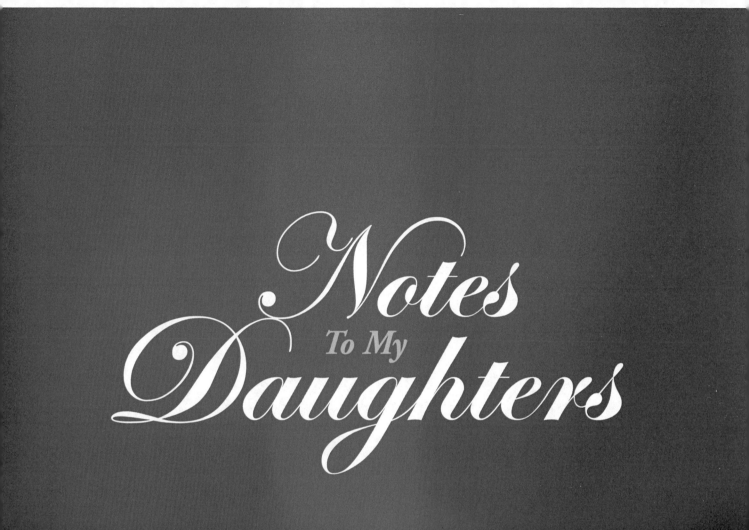

Notes To My Daughters

Rene Salzman

Balboa Press books may be ordered through booksellers or by contacting:

Balboa Press
A Division of Hay House
1663 Liberty Drive
Bloomington, IN 47403
www.balboapress.com
1 (877) 407-4847

ISBN: 978-1-4525-8870-4 (sc)
ISBN: 978-1-4525-8871-1 (e)

Library of Congress Control Number: 2013922959

Printed in the United States of America.

Balboa Press rev. date: 12/27/2013

BALBOA.
PRESS
A DIVISION OF HAY HOUSE

Prologue

I wrote this book for my daughters who truly have
my heart. They will travel in many directions until
they become the women that I know they can
be. I give them these words as a common sense
path so they can breathe easier on their way.

Mom

*A*ll anyone wants is to feel a sense
of belonging and to matter.

*K*now who you are, so you don't
keep waiting for others to tell you.

*H*ave your own life so you are interesting
and not a parasite in your marriage.

*M*arriage is a roller coaster. In the down times, try
to remember all the good stuff. Put memories in the bank.

$\mathcal{E}$ach phase of your life can be an adventure.
Your attitude will determine if it is a fun one.

*L*ife is not true confessions.

*M*ake your spouse feel adored, and looked after. That will come back to you.

$\mathcal{Y}$our spouse should always be important
in your life. Children leave and then you have
to go back to just looking at each other.

*L*et your children know that you
adore their "significant other" until they
don't. Only your children matter.

$\mathcal{D}$on't get invested in other people's situations. Make sure you don't care about what's happening more than they do. This is especially true if your children are involved.

*D*on't act like his mother. Men
don't want to fuck their mothers.

*M*en and women fight differently. Don't
fight mean and dirty even if they do.

*E*very marriage has an unwritten and unspoken agreement. Just know it and accept it. Don't talk about it.

*M*en sometimes "don't get it". Don't expect them to.

*A*pologize. It's not always important that someone has to "win". Keeping peace and letting him feel like a winner works. Small things don't matter. Fight on the bigger issues.

*G*et your feelings out. Anger comes out as snide remarks and can get nasty when not voiced.

*Y*our mouth might be saying one thing, but what is the underlining message you are really saying?

*D*on't "fix" or remedy all your children's problems. Soon they won't know how to do it themselves. They need to learn and feel capable.

$\mathcal{B}$ad experiences happen in life. See what you can learn and change about yourself. Turn it into a life changing positive experience. Take responsibility for your part in the shit that happened.

Remember that everyone has to walk their own path to become who they are meant to be.

$\mathcal{Y}$ou may wish that he can read your mind and "just do it". No one can. Give that up. Be clear on your needs. You will have less disappointment.

*S*tay with people that add to your life. Not those who take and chip away from it.

*L*ife is all about making choices. Think before you act. It really does affect your life.

*I*f the man in your life goes on a rant, just sing in your head. Don't take it personally. They need to vent. It might have nothing to do with you.

*M*arry for laughter. He might eventually get bald and fat, but you will always laugh together.

*W*ork on yourself until you really see your inner beauty. Then you will feel the calmness and truly believe in yourself.

*A*lways have a hidden stash of money from your husband. Totally disgusting to always ask for money.

You have a father and mother for a reason. Know it is really ok with me when you need just your dad to work a situation out. Moms are not the end all.

$\mathcal{P}$eople let criticisms out of their mouths very easily. It seems harder to give compliments. Giving compliments makes them and you feel good.

*S*aying, "I love you" and complimenting people should be given free. Don't give with the expectation of getting it back.

*M*en and women react to situations
differently. Allow it. It's life.

*K*eep the drama in your accessories
and not in your life.

*T*ry to look your best every day. If you feel like shit, you probably look like shit. Put some makeup on.

*L*ook at the man on the dance floor. The one who moves his hips the best, is usually good in bed.

*A*lways appreciate a present even before you open it. Presents stop if you don't.

*I*f a relative bothers you, make believe they are a stranger. You will treat them better for the moment.

*M*ake your home a safe haven.
The world can be mean.

The woman is the root of the tree. Stay grounded and positive. Your family can flourish then.

*P*ick a mate that makes you giggle and adores you. Everything else falls into place.

$\mathcal{M}$y wedding vows: To love, respect
and give each other room to grow.

*A*lways be his arm candy. Don't wait to be the second wife before you realize you have to look good every day.

*N*ever give him back change.

*M*en can hire a housekeeper. They need a wife.

*G*ive compliments. Men like them too.

$\mathcal{D}$on't be a "Boo". That's the person who sees the negative and the worst in situations. It is not only sucky but takes the good energy from the room.

*R*emember that before you ask a salesperson for advice, that everyone has their own idea of what looks pretty.

*D*on't wait or expect someone else to make you happy. Always have an inner cheerleader.

*D*on't look at other couples for what a marriage should be like. Every couple should figure out what works for them.

*L*ooking at life idealistically sets you up
for disappointments, being an optimistic
realist will keep a smile on your face.

*I*t is important to know what you are good at, as well as what you are not good at.

Printed in the United States
By Bookmasters